Suzuki® Violin School
VIOLIN PART
VOLUME 7

Copyright © 1978 Dr. Shinichi Suzuki
Sole publisher for the world except Japan:
Summy-Birchard, Inc.
All Rights Reserved   Printed in U.S.A.

Summy-Birchard Inc.
exclusively distributed by
Warner Bros. Publications Inc.
15800 N.W. 48th Avenue
Miami, Florida 33014

ISBN 0-87487-156-5

The Suzuki name, logo and wheel
are trademarks of Dr. Shinichi Suzuki used under
exclusive license by Summy-Birchard, Inc.

INTRODUCTION

FOR THE STUDENT: This material is part of the worldwide Suzuki Method of teaching. Companion recordings should be used with these publications. In addition, there are piano accompaniment books that go along with this material.

FOR THE TEACHER: In order to be an effective Suzuki teacher, a great deal of ongoing education is required. Your national Suzuki association provides this for its membership. Teachers are encouraged to become members of their national Suzuki associations and maintain a teacher training schedule, in order to remain current, via institutes, short and long term programs. You are also encouraged to join the International Suzuki Association.

FOR THE PARENT: Credentials are essential for any teacher that you choose. We recommend you ask your teacher for his or her credentials, especially listing those relating to training in the Suzuki Method. The Suzuki Method experience should be a positive one, where there exists a wonderful, fostering relationship between child, parent and teacher. So choosing the right teacher is of the utmost importance.

In order to obtain more information about the Suzuki Method, please contact your country's Suzuki Association, the International Suzuki Association at 3-10-15 Fukashi, Matsumoto City 390, Japan, The Suzuki Association of the Americas, 1900 Folsom, #101, Boulder, Colorado 80302, or Summy-Birchard Inc., c/o Warner Bros. Publications, 15800 N.W. 48th Avenue, Miami, FL 33014, for current Associations' addresses.

CONTENTS

(Nos. 5 and 6 are unaccompanied)

1 Minuet
メヌエット

W. A. Mozart
モーツァルト

Allegretto

基本練習

Fundamental Exercise: **Grundlegende Übung:**
Exercice Fondamental: *Ejercicio Fundamental:*

2da volta rit. . . . . . Minuet D. C.

各弦の練習もおこなう。
Practice the same on the other strings, too.
Faire le même exercice sur les autres cordes.
Das Gleiche auch auf den anderen Saiten üben.
Practique lo mismo en las otras cuerdas también.

2 Courante

クーラント

A. Corelli
コレルリ

2・3の指によるトリルの練習をゆっくり正確によくお
こなうこと。

Practice the above trills slowly and exactly.

Exercer les trilles ci-dessus lentement et exactement.

Die obigen Trillernoten langsam und genau üben.

Practique los trinos de arriba despacio y exactamente.

3 Sonata No. 1
ソナタ第一番

G. F. Handel
ヘンデル

4th position
4ème position
vierte Lage
4ta posición

3rd position
3ème position
dritte Lage
tercera posición

diminuendo

2nd position
2ème position
zweite Lage
2da posición

Elementary Practice for Concerto No. 1

「コンチェルト第1番」の　基本練習

Exercice élémentaire pour le "Concerto No. 1"
Grundlegende Übung für "Konzert Nr. 1"
Práctica elementaria para «Concierto Núm. 1»

つぎのＡＢＣ記号はバイオリンパートの各ＡＢＣのとこ
ろの基本練習です。

The following elementary exercises marked with A, B, C, are for the parts in the score marked with the corresponding letters.

Les exercices de base suivants marqués A, B, C sont pour les parties de la partition marquées des lettres correspondantes.

Die folgenden grundlegenden, mit A, B, C gekennzeichneten Übungen sind für die Teile im Notenblatt, die mit den entsprechenden Buchstaben markiert sind.

Los siguientes ejercicios elementarios marcados con A, B, C son para las partes en la partitura marcadas con las correspondientes letras.

The First Movement

第一楽章

Le Premier Mouvement　　***Erster Satz***　　El Primer Movimiento

弓中央から弓巾小さく

Draw a short stroke from the middle of the bow.
Donner un coup d'archet court en commençant au milieu de l'archet.

Einen kurzen Strich von der Mitte des Bogens ziehen.
Haga un golpe corto desde la mitad del arco.

ゆっくりと、しかしポジションの用意は速く、正確な音程でひく。

Play slowly with correct intonation and with quick preparation for the shifts.

Jouer lentement avec une intonation juste, et avec une préparation rapide des positions.

Spiele langsam in den genauen Tonhöhen und mit schneller Vorbereitung des Lagenwechsels.

Toque lentamente con afinación buena, y con preparación rápida para cambiar la posición.

2 の指に 3 をつける
Place the 3rd finger close to the 2nd.
Placer le 3ème doigt près du 2ème.
Setze den dritten Finger nahe neben den zweiten.
Coloque el tercer dedo cerca del segundo.

The Second Movement

第二楽章

Le deuxième mouvement   *Der zweite Satz*   El Segundo Movimiento

A 弦.だけ 、
Play on the A string alone.
Jouer uniquement sur la corde du la.
Spiele nur auf der A-Saite.
Toque solamente en la cuerda la.

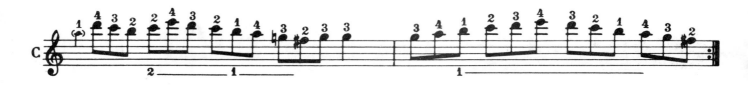

The Third Movement

第三楽章

Le Troisième Mouvement   ***Der dritte Satz***   El Tercer Movimiento

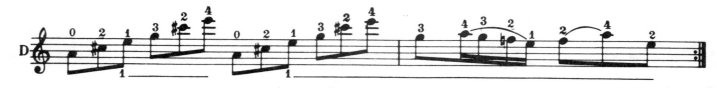

† ＊ と記したのは前の音との間隔を示す。†は一音の間
隔、＊は半音、㋕は指を近くつけた位置であることを示
す。

The mark † or ＊ shows the interval from the preceding tone; † means a whole tone interval and ＊ a semitone. ²⁄₃] indicates a position where these two fingers should be placed closely together.

Das Zeichen † oder ＊ zeigt das Intervall vom vorhergehenden Ton; † zeigt ein Ganzton-Intervall und ＊ ein ein Halbton. ²⁄₃] zeigt eine Lage an, wo diese zwei Finger dicht nebeneinande gesetzt werden sollen.

La marque † ou ＊ montre la nature de l'intervalle entre le ton précédent et le nouveau ton; † signifie un intervalle d'un ton entier et ＊ signifie un intervalle d'un demi-ton. ²⁄₃] indique une position dans laquelle ces deux doigts doivent être placés très près l'un de l'autre.

La marca † o ＊ muestra el intervalo desde el tono precedente; † significa un intervalo de tono entero y ＊ un semitono. ²⁄₃] indica una posición en cual estos dos dedos se deben colocar juntos.

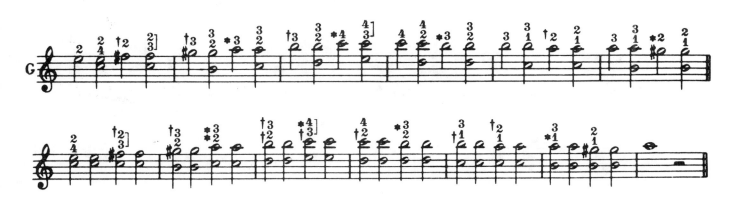

4 Concerto No. 1

コンチェルト第一番

J. S. Bach
バッハ

18

Allegro assai

5 Gigue

ジーグ

J. S. Bach
バッハ

6 Courante

クーラント

J. S. Bach
バッハ

Fundamental Exercise:
Practice for playing fifths simultaneously.

Exercice fondamental:
S'exercer à jouer les cinqs simultanément.

五度を同時に押える練習

Grundlegende Übung:
Übe, Quinten gleichzeitig zu spielen.

Ejercicio Fundamental:
Práctica para tocar quintas simultaneamente.

7 Allegro
アレグロ

A. Corelli
コレルリ

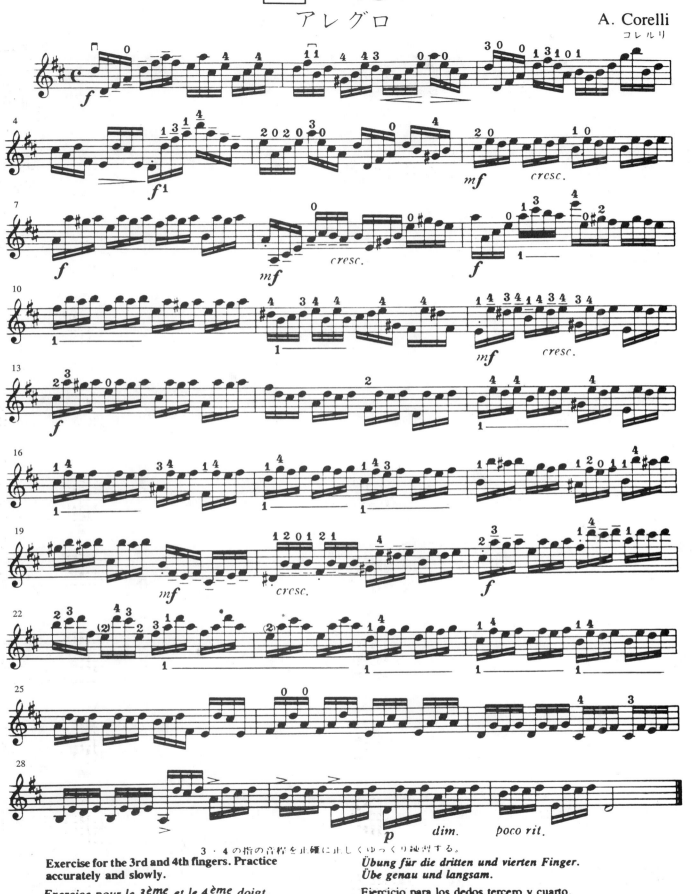

3・4の指の音程を正確に正しくゆっくり練習する。

Exercise for the 3rd and 4th fingers. Practice
accurately and slowly.

Übung für die dritten und vierten Finger.
Übe genau und langsam.

Exercice pour le 3ème et le 4ème doigt.
S'exercer lentement et correctement.

Ejercicio para los dedos tercero y cuarto.
Practique en forma exacta y lentamente.

23